THE PICNIC TABLE

This is a true story ....

We went a ride upon our bikes
To enjoy the open air.
A few miles north of Nottingham
I forget exactly where.

We went for miles, my wife and I
Along a cycle track.
When lunchtime came, we tried to find
A place to have our snack.

Eventually we came upon
A proper picnic place,
With benches place strategic'ly
Around an open space.

The seats were those quite common now,
With table/bench combined.
Sev'ral were already full
Of families, reclined.

They watched as we got off our bikes
And unpacked all our gear.
We set the table – tea and buns,
Some cake, a can of beer.

Before we settled down to eat,
Our bikes we did attend.
Against the table they were propped,
One at either end.

We were at last ready to eat.
We sat down side by side.
We were both eager for a meal
After our long ride.

But that was not to be, alas,
For what we quickly found,
The empty seats across from us
Slowly left the ground.

We should have sat down one each side
And spread our weight around
But normally these picnic seats
Are firmly bolted down.

The whole contraption slowly tipped,
And much to our unease,
The contents of the table top
Landed on our knees.

We came to rest upon our backs,
The table in the air,
With sandwiches and plastic cups
And cake strewn ev'rywhere.

Our troubles were not over yet;
Our bikes, propped either end,
Fell underneath the table's legs.
It could not now descend.

The other folk around the place
Enjoyed the cabaret.
When they sat down, they didn't expect
An acrobat display.

And all the while, they laughed at us,
And savoured our demise,
We lay there kicking on our backs
Just like two dying flies.

Eventually, we wriggled out
And managed to get free,
Then clambered from amongst the cakes,
And sandwiches and tea.

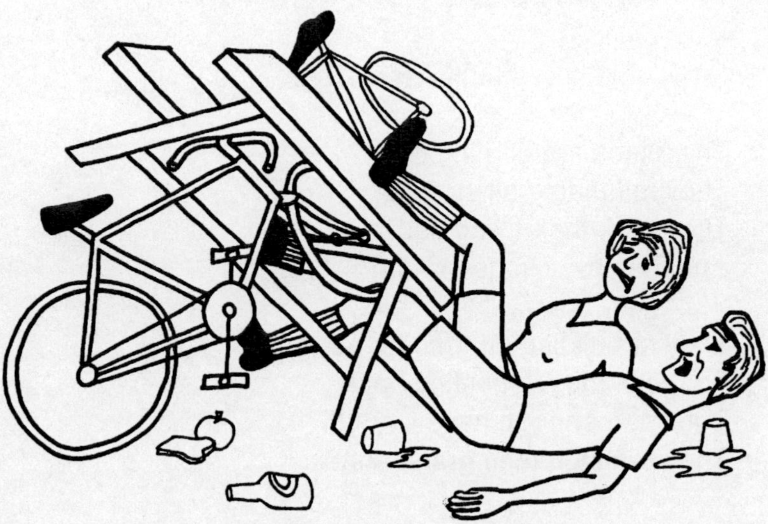

We dusted off the bread and crisps
As best as we were able.
Then struggled to extract our bikes
From underneath the table.

We got it all back into place
And tried to look serene.
We calmly did the best we could
To restore the tranquil scene.

But it was really not the same
Surrounded by debris,
With half a sandwich each – squashed flat
And trousers soaked in tea.

☺☺☺☺☺☺☺☺☺☺☺☺☺☺☺☺☺☺☺☺

BEWARE !!!

The aliens are coming.
They're landing all around.
They park their flying saucers
And then they go to ground.

They're building up their numbers,
For now, they're holding back,
But when enough have landed,
They'll launch their grand attack.

But nobody has noticed
All their abandoned craft,
Because they're very cunning;
These aliens are not daft.

Each saucer that transports them
From some far distant star
Is simply made to look like
The wheel-trim from a car.

They streak across the light years,
Along the Milky Way,
And land upon our verges
In thousands, ev'ry day.

We take them all for granted
Those shiny silver discs.
It's time we all began to
Appreciate the risks.

Just think how many wheel-trims
You see from day to day,
Far more than you see wheels
Where one has gone astray.

We think they come from Vauxhall,
From Rover or from Ford,
But they have come much further
With aliens on board.

Next time you see a wheel-trim
Just lying by the road,
Attack it and destroy it
Before it can unload.

And if someone should see you,
And ask you, "What's up mate?"
Tell them they must do likewise
Before it's all too late.

☺☺☺☺☺☺☺☺☺☺☺☺☺☺☺☺☺☺☺☺☺☺☺☺

JUST NONSENSE

A ram and a dog
Went out in the fog,
And far and away they did roam.
Said the dog to the ram,
"I can't see where I am,
We're lost and I want to go home."

They then met a frog,
While out in the fog,
And he knew which way they should go.
"You are in a jam",
Said the frog to the ram,
"Follow me, but I only go slow."

They went through a bog,
The ram, dog and frog.
They were lucky not to be drowned.
Then along came a tram,
And the dog, frog and ram,
Rode all the way home for a pound.

☺☺☺☺☺☺☺☺☺☺☺☺☺☺☺☺☺☺☺☺☺☺☺☺

MAKE IT RHYME

M any modern poems
A re not designed to rhyme.
K eeping to tradition,
E ntails a lot of time.

I t's easy to write lyrics
T hat end with any sound.

R hyming on the other hand,
H as to be profound.
Y es, each and every line,
M ust readily combine,
E nhancing the design.

☺☺☺☺☺☺☺☺☺☺☺☺☺☺☺☺☺☺☺☺

SHADOWS

I feel quite sad for shadows,
Their life can't be much fun.
No matter how they move about,
They never see the sun.

I'm sure they'd like to sunbathe
When it's a sunny day,
But they just know that someone
Is always in the way.

They're pulled out long and thin sometimes,
And then they're short and fat.
They've only two dimensions.
I don't think I'd like that.

They have to do what we do.
They've no choice of their own.
Although they must get quite fed up,
You never hear them moan.

If I were someone's shadow,
I think I'd get quite stressed,
At least, when it is raining,
They have some time to rest.

☺☺☺☺☺☺☺☺☺☺☺☺☺☺☺☺☺☺☺☺

CHIPS

"Chip and Pin" is here to stay.
I need a number now to pay.
Forget my name, it is no use,
Four digits I must now produce.

I have to choose which will be mine.
My date of birth will do just fine.
"No don't choose that", is the advice,
"Fraudsters will guess it in a trice".

I have a PIN with my bank card.
Make this the same; that can't be hard,
But then the powers-that-be say, "Look,
That makes it easy for the crook.

If they get one, they'll have them all
And through your savings they will trawl
Different numbers must be used
So that the thieves remain confused."

But I'm confused, ne'er mind the crook,
I'll write them all down in a book.
"Oh no you don't!", the experts say,
"Suppose you lose your book one day.

Just keep the numbers in your head."
But that is something easy said,
My memory's no longer new,
And numbers tend to fall straight through.

And now a new source of concern,
For pass<u>words</u> I must choose and learn.
I phone the bank - and then the test,
My password is their first request.

What did I tell them it would be?
What word did I choose as the key?
I quote them one but that won't do,
I ask if I could have a clue.

And now the internet's arrived,
Passwords galore must be derived.
I need a word just to log on
Before I contact anyone.

I pay my gas bill on the net,
I need a password – don't forget.
And then for the electric bill,
I must have yet another still.
And ev'ry company I choose,
A brand new password I must use.

But internet banking is the tops,
It's worse than all the on-line shops.

When I joined up I had a PIN,
A number with 10 digits in;
A system which could well provide
Enough for ev'ryone alive.

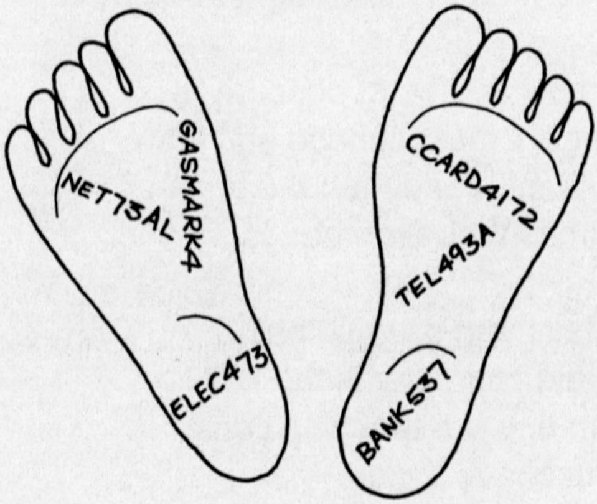

At last I've found a way to cheat,
I've had them tattooed on my feet.

☺☺☺☺☺☺☺☺☺☺☺☺☺☺☺☺☺☺☺☺☺☺☺

A DOG'S VIEW

My name is Rags, I am a dog,
Please listen to my monologue.
My owner's causing me concern
And I'm not sure which way to turn.

Please understand, she is a dear,
We've been together many a year,
But she has started recently
Behaving oddly – as you'll see.

She takes me down the avenue
To do what all dogs have to do,
But when I've done, what do I find?
She picks up what I've left behind.

She has a bag to help retrieve it
And brings it home. Can you believe it?
It's quite disgusting, wouldn't you say?
She always does it, ev'ry day.
Explain to me – a Labrador,
What could she possibly want it for?

I've tried to do it out of sight
But then she'll search with all her might
And if I distribute it round
She makes quite sure it's all been found

It's very odd, don't you agree.
Why does she do it? Please tell me.
What will she do with all that stuff,
And when will she have got enough?

☺☺☺☺☺☺☺☺☺☺☺☺☺☺☺☺☺☺☺☺

A SURPRISE IN THE NIGHT

This is another true story. As you read it, you will realise that I could not possibly have invented such a tale. In his defence, I wish to point out that my son was only 17 at the time.

Our younger son had passed his test
And now he had a car.
It's touring days were long since passed.
It didn't travel far.

He passed first time and we were proud
But what did not appeal,
Our little lad out on the road,
Behind a steering wheel.

We lay awake in bed each night,
While he was on the town,
Waiting 'til he rattled home
And we could settle down.

But worst of all was dropping off,
Then waking – full of doubt,
Not knowing if he had come back
Or if he was still out.

We'd lie there wond'ring where he was.
We'd listen for his tread.
And when we finally went to look,
He's fast asleep in bed.

One night we lay there yet again
Tired out but wide awake.
We heard him come into the drive,
And then pull on his brake.

He slammed his car door shut so hard,
It gave us quite a shock.
We listened as his front door key
Rattled in the lock.

He came into the hallway
But then it all went still.
He stopped and stood there quietly,
We thought that he was ill.

At last he shouted up the stairs,
Some words we'll ne'er forget,
"Dad – I've killed a badger."
He sounded quite upset.

I spent some time just thinking
Of a suitable reply,
But, before my thoughts I'd gathered,
Came another plaintive cry.

"I've brought it home," he shouted,
"I have it in the car."
......Now there's a situation,
Somewhat irregular!!

In the early hours of morning,
A thing you can't ignore,
What to do with a badger
Delivered to your door.

"What can I do now", I said
"While lying here in bed?
Take the thing out of your car
And put it in the shed."

After lots of shuffling
As round and round he crept,
At last he came upstairs to bed
And settled down and slept.

But we were wide awake by then
With badgers on our mind,
Thinking of the morning time,
And what we would then find.

And what if it recovered
Whilst lying in the shed,
Our son had no experience
Of badgers that were dead.

At last fatigue o'ercame us
And we dropped off to sleep,
Counting piles of badgers
Instead of counting sheep.

Next morning came too quickly.
My first call was the shed.
I opened the door slowly,
My heart was filled with dread.

Now badgers I had seen afar
But close, they're twice as big.
This one was just enormous,
It looked more like a pig.

At least it wasn't prowling round,
I poked it with a stick.
It didn't move. Sure if it had,
I would have gone - real quick.

I tried to move it just a bit.
It was a heavy beast.
A badger is a hefty weight,
Especially when deceased.

It filled the shed, and smelled as well,
And probably had fleas.
I also think that badgers carry
All sorts of disease.

What could we do with such a thing?
We couldn't just cremate it.
It wouldn't fit into the bin,
And Oxfam wouldn't take it.

We thought about it long and hard
And came to a decision,
Take it back to where it died,
The site of the collision.

It took some lifting, it was fat,
Smelly and hirsute.
We dragged it back up to the car
And stowed it in the boot.

Our son drove off in early light,
Before the world could see.
His speeding car concluded
The badger tragedy.

So if you kill a badger
Don't get into a tizz.
Don't pick it up and bring it home,
Just leave it where it is.

☺☺☺☺☺☺☺☺☺☺☺☺☺☺☺☺☺☺

NURSERY RHYMES

Little Miss Muffit
Sat on her tuffet.
But who was Miss Muffitt?
And what is a tuffet?
Could she have been Clare
And sat on a chair?
If she had been French,
She'd have sat on a bench.
If her name had been Mabel,
She'd have sat at the table.
But no, she was Muffit
And made do with a tuffet.

Jack and Jill went up the hill
For water in a pail.
But wells are never up a hill,
They're always down a dale.
You don't get water up a hill,
It's always at the bottom,
A basic fact of gravity
Which Jack must have forgotten.

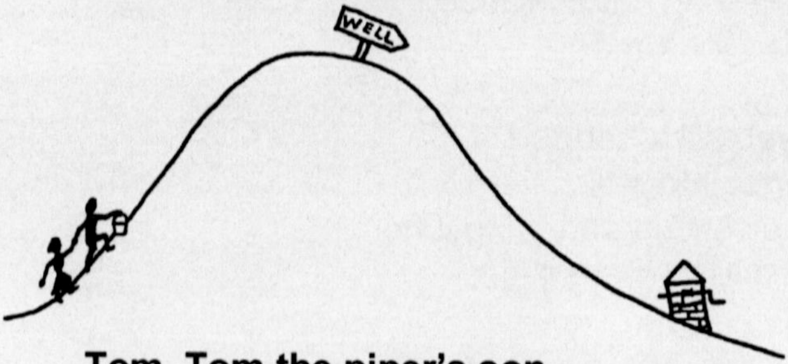

Tom, Tom the piper's son
Stole a pig and away did run.
The pig was eat
And Tom was beat
And Tom went crying down the street.
He told the police and showed his bruise
And his dad was arrested for child abuse.

Sing a song of sixpence
A pocket full of rye.
Four and twenty blackbirds baked in a pie.
When the pie was opened,
The birds began to sing.
After baking in an oven
They wouldn't sing a thing.

Three blind mice.
Three blind mice.
Why say it twice?
Why say it twice?
Once would suffice.
Once would suffice.

Ring a ring of roses,
A pocket full of posies,
Atishoo, atishoo,
Now go and wipe your noses.

Little Jack Horner
Sat in a corner.
Again, just like Muffit,
Who sat on her tuffet,
He only found fame
Because of his name,
And he gained his renown
From the place he sat down.
His brother-in-law
Could have sat on the floor,
While his great Uncle Fred
Would have just gone to bed.
At least he had sense
Not to sit on the fence.

Humpty Dumpty sat on a wall,
Hadn't he any sense at all?
He should have asked Muffit
For a seat on her tuffet.

If I were an egg, I'd take good care
To only sit down on a very low chair.
And I'd put cushions all over the place
And a really thick carpet --- just in case.

☺☺☺☺☺☺☺☺☺☺☺☺☺☺☺☺☺☺☺☺

HAPPY BIRTHDAY FROM GRANDAD

Birthdays are an awkward time for grandads,
We have to buy the kids some sort of gift,
But we have no idea what they're wanting,
And in this modern world, we are adrift.

I asked my teenage grandson what he wanted.
He told me but I didn't understand,
Half the words he used I hadn't heard of,
It's like visiting a strange and foreign land.

He said he'd like an iPod from an Apple,
With earbuds and a six four megglebite ram,
And it has to handle m-pegs, that's essential.
I came away, my mind was in a jam.

I asked if he would like a nice Meccano,
With lots of nuts and bolts and strips of steel.
He could build a nice big crane, or make a lorry;
His face suggested this did not appeal.

He talked about a new flap-top computer,
With gigglebites of mem'ry and a mouse.
I told him that I didn't think his mother
Would want a furry animal in the house.

I said an Airfix kit may be the answer.
He could make a plastic model to admire.
He could build a World War II Lancaster bomber,
And hang it from the ceiling on a wire.

A mobile phone was what he really wanted,
A 3G one of course which downloads tunes,
With bluetooth and a megapixie camera,
And lots of games for rainy afternoons.

I explained the possibilities of plywood.
A fretwork set would surely suit him fine.
He could make his mum a toast-rack or a jigsaw.
I told him of the fun I'd had with mine.

He said that he would rather have an X-box.
The new 360 is the best by far,
It must include two wireless controllers,
With teraflops of speed and PGR.

This present wasn't getting any closer,
X box, iPod, m-pegs, blue tooth, 3G phone,
It's lucky there's a universal language,
It's called "money" – then he can buy his own!

☺☺☺☺☺☺☺☺☺☺☺☺☺☺☺☺☺☺☺☺

THE GREATEST INVENTION

It is a subject of debate
That tests the greatest mind,
What is the most amazing thing
Invented by mankind?

Some say, “It is the wheel, of course,
For, if it wasn’t there,
We’d have no cars, no clocks, no bikes,
We’d just walk ev’rywhere.”

Some say, “It is the printing press.”
While others say the jet.
The bow and arrow impress some,
So does the Internet.

While all these things are very good,
One winner I declare.
It’s something often overlooked.
It is the humble chair.

Before the chair I bet the folk
Forever wore a frown.
Imagine living in a world
With nowhere to sit down.

You’d have to stand or go to bed,
Or lie upon the floor.
You could just kneel down I suppose,
But you would soon be sore.

You’d have to stand to eat your meals,
If chairs had never been;
You couldn’t sit to watch TV,
Or read a magazine.

And all those useful high-up shelves,
You'd have to just abandon,
For you would never reach up there
Without a chair to stand on.

There'd be no seats inside your car,
Just one big empty space.
You'd have to fasten yourself down
Or bounce around the place.

There'd be no paliamentr'y seats,
Back-benchers, nor Church pews,
No deckchairs and no chairpersons
Not even sit-down loos.

So give the chair its due respect.
It may seem quite humdrum,
But it is so much more than just
Somewhere to park your bum.

NEIGH-BOURS

"A nasty cough you've there,"
Said the stallion to the mare.
"No offence of course,
But you're sounding rather ***hoarse***."
She went on to explain,
"I've been standing in the ***rein***.
Through puddles I have paddled,
With this cough I am now ***saddled***.
If you ask me out today,
I'm afraid I must say '***neigh***',
I shiver and I dither,
And I'm quite under the ***wither***.

To recover, I'm unable.
My condition is un-***stable***.
I cannot eat my feed,
I must go without in-***steed***.

If my voice should crack and falter,
It's something I can't ***halter***
My sneeze I can't control,
I feel a proper ***foal***.
But I still refuse to quit,
I'll be better in a ***bit***."

☺☺☺☺☺☺☺☺☺☺☺☺☺☺☺☺☺☺☺☺☺☺

SOME LIMERICKS

A young man in weather forecasting
Wore clothes of colours contrasting.
On bright sunny days
His gaudy displays
Were frequently quite flabbergasting.

There was a young man from Doncaster
Who drove his car faster and faster.
He smashed through some cones
And broke several bones
And now he's all covered in plaster.

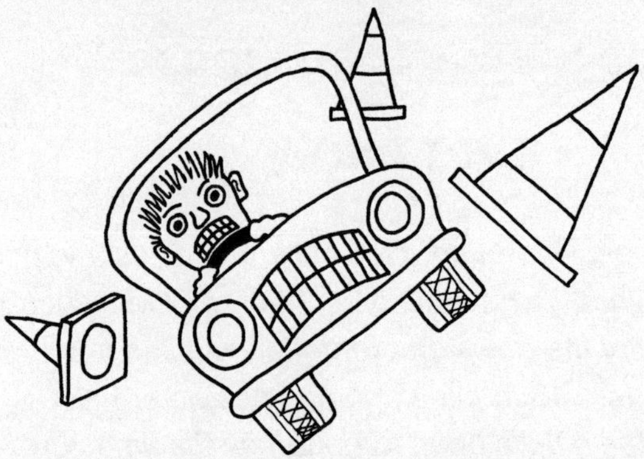

There was a young man called Tchaikowsky
While walking, he took his coat off-sky
But the wind blew quite chill,
And he became ill,
The doctor diagnosed whooping cough-sky

Young Barry was quite a fanatic,
His opinions were very dogmatic.
One day he saw red,
His wife turned and said,
"Don't be so melodramatic!"

☺☺☺☺☺☺☺☺☺☺☺☺☺☺☺☺☺☺☺☺

EMPTY NOW

Usually, a poem written on a topical subject has a very limited life. When I wrote this one, I thought the subject would be out of the news and forgotten within a few weeks. That was 18 months ago and people are still leaving regularly. If it's been forgotten by the time you read this book, I apologise.

It used to be full of voices and noise,
A building alive with both sorrows and joys,
The echoes of laughter, the rattle of spoons,
The occasional snoring on warm afternoons.
But slowly the people have all gone away,
Their numbers have dwindled with each passing day.
The last one to leave has now said his goodbye.
He went with no tear, not even a sigh.
The windows now cheerless, the doors all ajar,
The folk who were here, have all travelled far.
The rooms are all silent, the air has a chill,
Sudbury Prison is empty and still.

DOWN IN THE DEPTHS

I think that I'm quite brave at times,
Some risky things I've tried,
But there's one phrase my wife will say
That leaves me petrified.

For when some item I require,
The words I dread to hear -
"It's in my handbag, help yourself".
They fill my heart with fear.

A handbag is a dreadful place
With secrets dark and low,
A labyrinth where mortal man
Should ne'er be asked to go.

A place for lipstick, scissors, keys
A purse and powder puff.
It's not a place for men to go,
It's full of woman stuff.

A mirror, pills and credit cards,
Pens which no longer write,
And deeper down all sorts of things
Which never see the light.

Some stamps, a pencil, glasses, comb,
Mascara and hair lacquer,
A miniature pack of playing cards
From last year's Christmas cracker.

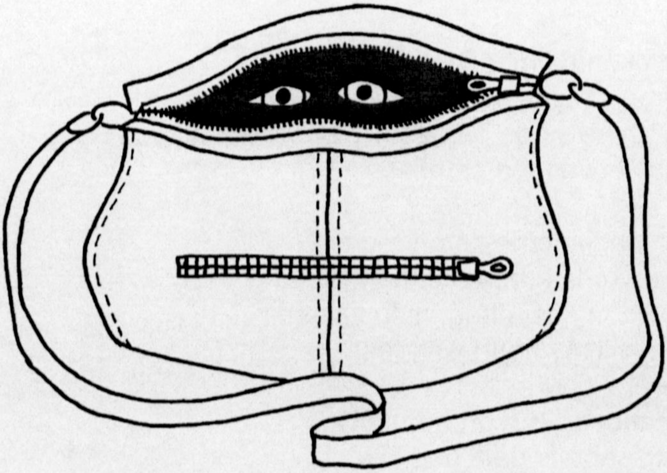

Some creased and dog-eared photographs
Still held in high regard,
And recipes obtained from friends
On tatty bits of card.

Forgotten sweets collecting fluff,
A charm to bring her luck.
Would you believe, the other day
I found a ration book!

☺☺☺☺☺☺☺☺☺☺☺☺☺☺☺☺☺☺